Contents

Parts of Animals

Our bodies are important

Our bodies let us do all sorts of amazing things! What are these children doing? Which parts of their bodies are they using?

Alison Lapper is an artist who paints with her mouth.

Things to do

Can you write your name holding your pencil between your toes?

Looking after our bodies

Some people use science to help us look after parts of our bodies.

An optician looks after our eyes.

A dentist helps us to look after our teeth.

A nurse helps to fix our bones when they are broken.

Who else helps us to keep our bodies healthy?

The senses

We have five senses. These senses help us to understand the world around us.

Can you name our senses?

Imagine what life would be like without one of your senses.

Did you know?

Butterflies taste through their feet.

Which is your favourite sense? Why?

Did you know?

Dogs can smell 100 000 times better than humans.

Animal parts

Some animal body parts are like our own and some look very different. Some have special names.

What are these animal body parts?

How many more animal parts can you think of?

Changing Seasons

Make it!

Follow the instructions to make a wind toy.
You will need:

scissors

a ruler

a lolly stick

tissue
paper

sticky tape

1. Cut 15 strips of tissue paper 30 cm long and 1 cm wide.

2. Cut a long piece of sticky tape and stick your strips to it.

3. Roll up the tape and stick your tissue streamers to the lolly stick.

Things to do
Try your wind toy outside on a windy day!

Spot the season!
Look at all the things you can spot in the different seasons.

Spring

Birds build their nests.

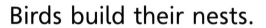

Buds and unfolding leaves appear on trees.

Frogs lay frogspawn in ponds.

Bluebells, primroses and daffodils grow.

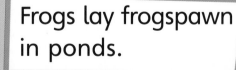

Summer

Young birds leave their nests.

Trees are covered in green leaves.

Wild flowers grow.

Bees, butterflies and other insects fly around. You can hear lots of buzzing and humming!

Autumn

Some birds migrate to other countries where it is warmer.

Leaves on some trees change colour from green to brown, orange, red and yellow.

You will see spiders, ladybirds, bees and wasps indoors trying to find warm places to live.

Winter

Some trees lose their leaves.

There are very few flowers, but you will see holly, ivy and mistletoe growing.

Animals are hard to see because they hibernate. You might be able to spot their footprints in the snow!

Things to do
How many other signs of the seasons can you find?

Spot the plants

Here is an allotment. An allotment is a garden. People grow fruits, vegetables, herbs and flowers in their allotments.

Look at the picture. How many plants can you name? How many do you eat?

cabbages

Plant parts

Read all about the different parts of plants.

Leaves can be different shapes and sizes.

We eat some stems. Some stems have sharp thorns to stop them being eaten!

We grow flowers because they are pretty. Some flowers smell nice too!

Dandelions have a single strong root. Trees have thick roots.

Trees are plants too

Yes, that's right! Trees are plants too!

Can you name the parts of this sycamore tree?

Which parts of the tree are these?

Things to do

We get wood from trees. Can you think of some things that we make from wood?

Comparing Materials

Make a sock creature

You will need:

- scissors
- glue
- different types of stuffing
- felt
- wool
- a sock
- stick-on eyes

1 Stick eyes onto your sock creature.

2 Cut out a felt mouth, nose and ears for your sock creature. Stick them on to finish the face.

3 Add wool for hair and felt arms and legs.

4 Choose some stuffing and stuff the sock.

5 Glue the open end of the sock together.

Old teddy bears

The first teddy bears were made nearly 120 years ago. They were made very differently then!

This bear was made over 100 years ago.

How were the first teddy bears made?

The first bears were made from a soft fur called mohair.

They had black leather eyes.

They were stuffed with sawdust.

I spy!
Look at these pictures of teddy bears. Can you see how their eyes have changed?

Things to do
Feel some sawdust. Do you think you would like a bear stuffed with it?

leather

glass

plastic

Science Skills

Investigate it!

Do all types of paper sink? Some children screwed up small pieces of paper. They put them in a bowl of water. They counted how long it took each piece of paper to start sinking.

Type of paper	Number counted to before the paper started to sink
Kitchen roll	5
Tissue	Floated
Toilet paper	2
Paper towel	15

This is what the children thought.

The toilet paper sank quickest.

All the papers sank.

The paper towel sank slowest.

Kitchen roll will be best for a toy boat.

Look at the table.
Are the children right?

Types of Animals

Animals everywhere
Animals are everywhere.
We keep some as pets.

We keep some on farms.

We can visit some animals in zoos.

Animals are all around us.

Things to do
How many animals can you spot today?

Chart it!

Class one voted for their favourite zoo animals. Here are their results.

Our favourite zoo animal

Animal	Number of votes
tiger	7
meerkat	10
elephant	6
camel	2
snake	3

They made a bar chart of their results.

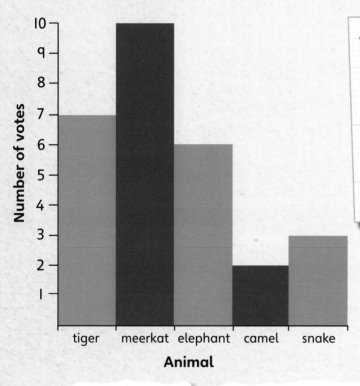

Things to do

- Can you make your own chart?
- What questions can your chart answer?

Which was their favourite animal?

How many children voted?

Which animal got six votes?

Animal ID

Scientists group animals by their similarities.

Mammals have hair or fur.

Birds have two legs, a beak and feathers.

Amphibians, like frogs, live on land and in water. They have moist skin and lay eggs.

Fish live in water. They have scales and fins. Gills help them to breathe underwater.

Reptiles have scaly skin. They lay their eggs on land.

Which group does this animal belong to?

Did you know?

Nearly one quarter of all mammals are bats.

Did you know?

The largest fish is the Whale Shark. It is 16 metres long!

A day in the life of a zookeeper

I feed the animals.

8:00 am

Time to clean up the poo!

9:00 am

I look after the sick animals.

1:00 pm

I talk to the visitors.

2:30 pm

Would you like to be a zookeeper?

26

Identifying Materials

A very useful powder

We use talcum powder to help dry damp skin. It has lots of other uses too!

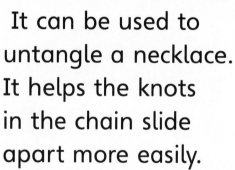

It can be used to untangle a necklace. It helps the knots in the chain slide apart more easily.

Things to do

Rub some butter on a rag. Sprinkle some talcum powder on the stain. Leave it for a few hours and brush the powder off. Has the stain gone?

Observe it!

Observing means looking, listening, smelling, tasting and touching things. Observing helps us to find out more about different things.

Look at these photographs. They have been taken very close to different materials. Can you guess which materials they are?

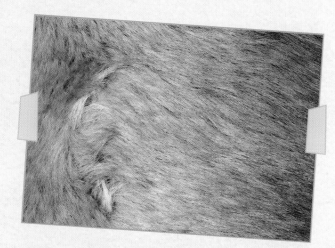

Is it a strange choice?

Would you make a chair out of jelly? Sometimes scientists and engineers make mistakes. They choose the wrong type of material to make things out of.

Find out

Can you find some other things made out of the wrong kinds of materials?

Years ago, a car called the Trabant was made in Germany. Some people thought it was made from cardboard! This wasn't true. It was made from cotton and resin which are also very weak. These cars fell apart if they crashed.

Index